RELEASE

The Winds of Ezekiel

PRAY

AUTHOR MALESSIA J. POE

AUTHOR MALESSIA J. POE
RUAH THE BREATH OF GOD, LLC.
Little Rock, Arkansas
www.lisapoeministries.wordpress.com
www.malessiajpoe.com

Printed in the United States of America

ISBN: 978-1-7356811-0-8

Unless otherwise noted, scripture quotations are taken from the King James Version Bible, Public Domain. Copyright 1973,1978,1984,2011 by Biblica, Inc. Used by permission. All rights reserved worldwide.

September 4, 2020

To my beloved brother, Joey, the master of chest, making so many master moves in your lifetime, I dedicate this book to you on your birthday September 4, 2020. You are truly missed. I love you.

Your Sister,
"Lisa"
~ Author Malessia J. Poe

TABLE OF CONTENTS

INTRODUCTION

Let the spirit of Ezekiel arise. The mantle is yet alive and remains to show forth the sovereignty of God. For we are the supreme beings from His creation, under His authority and His control. We are the good pleasure of God, being His children. We are the facts of life that God created to stand up and rule here in the world. For we are the universe in its entirety. We must know that God is concerned about our smallest even unto our greatest problems.

Let us **SPEAK** from the grounds of gravity launching our faith to travel beyond the sky and stars, grasping His sovereignty. Take a moment and breathe the sovereignty of God, The Almighty. We are royalty, ranking high, claiming our position, to send forth the CPR of God to resuscitate all emergencies, to cause the wind to blow, using the method from God's word. His breath has caused us to breathe.

Let the winds of God circulate from heart to heart and from chest to chest, moving prayer as the circle to revolve the unsolved problems. *Let us circle the earth with much prayer. Luke 12:48 says* that we are held responsible to stand up and fight the good fight of faith on our behalf and on the behalf of others as we pray, releasing the winds that will benefit the universe; to solve problems just as we use math to measure the fractions.

To whom much is given much will be required. Therefore, we will not be afraid, knowing that we are the chosen remnant and that we walk in the supernatural power of God!

Jesus left this powerful statement unto His disciples; "Behold I am with you." The Greater One, Jesus Christ released His winds upon them for them to be able to take and turn a whole world upside down, transferring the winds that fell on them on the day of Pentecost. Let us use the fraction of the word of God to slash any situation and become the denominator to bring prayer to the universe and to make us whole. ***THE WINDS OF PENTECOST.***

II Chronicles 7:14 says, "If my people", as God speaks unto us as being His people which are called by His name. Yes, God has a name and that name is Jesus. John 14:8 says, "Phillip saith unto Him, Lord shew us the Father, and it sufficeth us. Jesus saith unto him, Have I been so long time with you, and yet hast thou not known me, Phillip? Remember the miracles. Remember the signs. Remember the wonders. For he, that hath seen me hath seen The Father, working in the spirit of oneness." ***KNOWING The Name and Applying The Name JESUS. It is all in the Name of Jesus.***

The work must continue. We must humble ourselves and pray. We must use The Name Jesus. It is mandatory that we seek God's face and get in the rotation and turn from our wicked ways. God made us a promise to then heal our land. ***BEING CALLED TO DO GREATER WORKS, PRAY.***

Isaiah 26:3

PRAYER

Thou will keep him in perfect peace, whose mind is stayed on thee: because he trusteth in thee.

Father we Thank you for the possession of **Peace**. For **Peace** is our portion. We claim it. We put a fresh hold on **Peace**. We will walk continuously day by day in **Peace**. For **Peace** will remain with us the rest of our course. *We will keep the mind that has been granted to us by letting the mind be in us which was*

also in Christ Jesus. We accept the Christ-like mind. Yes Lord!

We will not be dismayed. For we trust our mind of *Peace*. We Thank you for giving us the establishment of **Peace**. For we are in our right minds. **Peace**. We come against the spirit of sabotage. **Peace!** We come against the spirit of Hidden Assassination. **Peace!** We Thank you for being a concerned God that has given us the power to develop **Peace**. ***In Jesus Name. Hallelujah! PEACE! DO NOT DISTURB. I HAVE GOD ON MIND. PEACE!***

The Work Zones of Winds

PRAYER

Father we Thank you for the number three that represents the Father, the Son, and the Holy ghost *being the trinity of oneness*. *WINDS*. I Thank you for the number five which represents the favor and grace of you. *WINDS*. We are the *Zones of Winds*. We send forth the *Local Winds*. We send forth the *High-Speed Winds*. We send forth the *Gust-Winds*. We release the *Duration Winds* to shift quickly to put asunder Satan and His works. *WINDS*. We call forth the *East Winds to depart our Red Sea.*

We now release the ***Winds of Good Health***. We call forth the ***WINDS*** to flow in the greater anointing. We call for the ***WINDS*** to adjust our appearance to see greater results. Now activate. Blow the ***WINDS*** from your mouth, ***RELEASING THE WORKZONE WINDS.***

Speaking Against Curses

PRAYER

Moving forward breaking generational cycles, we breathe the inheritance of the earth, being from the resurrection of Jesus Christ. His blood brings us into His covenant. We are covered by the blood. We Thank you LORD for coming and cleansing our bloodline. Our bloodlines will not be torn into pieces. For we are your masterpieces. ***Glory Hallelujah.*** We will shake the dust of stigma. ***Glory Hallelujah.*** Our bloodline will not die but live. We come against any negative traditions. It stops now at our bloodlines today. We represent the cut-off notice, commanding *in the Name of Jesus Christ.* High blood pressure, heart diseases, mental illness, alcohol abuse, and drug addiction, we command you to be detached as we fight for our rights, *In the Name of Jesus.* We will no longer feel rejection. Jesus paid it all at Calvary. We are whole. We are better. We believe therefore we will rise as we call out our names. *Shout over your generation in Jesus Name!*

For we are validated to bind and to loose. We walk with new keys. We are released and freed for our generations to come. *FREEDOM. SELAH.*

We Are the Delight of God!

PRAYER

We worship you for your mercy and your greatness. We behold your love. You are the Heavens unto us. How grateful are we. We are grateful for your delight to create us into being. We are the delight of God. We Thank you for interruptions that cause us to pause and give more attention unto you! We Thank you for blocking death seen and unseen. We are the delight of God.

We take each day, day by day, knowing that we are the delight of God. As we merge our hearts, it grants more desires to be in your presence. For we are the delight of you, The Almighty God. We are the delight of God.

All Is Well

PRAYER

Miracles are yet to be performed, using the powerful tool of prayer, in the lab creating a sound that goes beyond the Heavens. We honor you for being our physician as we lift our faith, walking in the spiritual revelation according to your word! Step up. Shift the atmosphere and release the word of God. For our steps to salvation have brought us unto you by faith. By faith we declare that *ALL IS WELL* as we take steps to our healing and our prosperity. We testify that *ALL IS WELL* as we worship you with our hands lifted, our banners of *ALL IS WELL* represent that Jehovah Nissi, The Lord, is our banner. We have advantage in knowing that *ALL IS WELL*. And it is so in Jesus's Mighty Name. We celebrate the defeat of our enemy. *ALL IS WELL. EXODUS 17.*

Matthew 24:13

PRAYER

We are standing on the word. ***Matthew 24:13 says,*** "But he that shall endure unto the end, the same shall be saved." We stand on the principle of your word, educating ourselves day by day. Your word has held us capable to stand in crisis. We dance before your throne, knowing the power of endurance, being called to endure.

We are called to renounce and proclaim that this will be the latter. We are the demand of greatness to endure. We undergo the suffering of this present moment to show what endurance looks like in difficult times. We are the force to cause hardships and problems to cease. We are the skills of God, to accomplish all things. ***ENDURANCE***

RHEMA

PRAYER

Father you have allowed our eyes to come open once again and we say Thank you. We Thank you for calling us beloved. We Thank you for wanting us to prosper and be in good health even as our souls shall prosper as according to ***III John 1:2***. We Thank you for wanting us to mount up with eagle wings. We Thank you for reigning within us. We know that you are a good Father who is assigned unto us, being your beloved children.

You have titled us as priest and royalty. You are the true meaning of a father. We Thank you because you did not cut us off. You were concerned about our promise. We your children come in many colors just as the rainbow made into an arch of colors. For we are the gold in your eyes. We Thank you for forming us from the dust of the earth. We are the reflection of God, being the Rhema of your word. We were already the daybreak of your sky. Rhema. We are here from the soil of God's Rhema.

PIERCE

PRAYER

We call the speed of the winds of God to come in and do battle. Battle on the behalf of ourselves and others in the name of The Lord Jesus. We use our word which is sharp. We stand firm with our feet standing on solid ground. Our domain is armed and dangerous from the spirit realm. We are the highest rank, ranking in the spirit. The weight of the word is girding our lives as we send the word at speeds, covering distance, as we release the wind and command our words to travel from the skills of our mouth, used to activate the task of wellness just as Jesus did. Jesus's Name will travel in the wind to battle in the schools, hospitals, nursing homes, and prisons. *"BE STILL AND KNOW THAT I AM GOD IN THE WINDS OF YOUR BATTLES."*

Radar Range

PRAYER

The radar of heaven will pick us up as we are praying across the countries, knowing that our prayers are reaching God. The radar will pick us up in the spirit to indicate that the radio waves have ascended and descended at the speed of lightning. We are the output of the radar, causing a movement of the new dimension. For our prayer is the atmosphere, 300,000 km per second. Look up and see the light. Our detection charges us to give Heaven the highest praise. ***Hallelujah***! We are the range of the radar enforcement, the maximum ranging radar. We log in day by day as the consign. We shift forward as we lift our cargo.

A Second Wind

Ezekiel Chapter 37:5 says, "Thus saith the Lord GOD unto these bones; Behold, I will cause breath to enter into you, and ye shall live:" Ezekiel was placed on an assignment by God, being put in the midst of a valley of dead bones. *WHEN YOU ARE CALLED TO AN ASSIGNMENT.* As he and God looked at the dead situation, God spoke unto him, informing him, "You are the only one that is left to speak life unto these dead bones. God stood in agreement with Ezekiel as they represented the number two, standing for the number of agreement.

God seen Himself when He looked and called Ezekiel, seeing His image and His likeness. For we have the breath of God which is the Ruah that God blew into us, man and we became a living soul. We represent the dust of the earth, breathing the breath of God.

Ezekiel, where went their hope? How in the world did they lose their sight in the valley? Here we are looking at a whole army that died out in a dry valley. Who did not pay attention when they seen the numbers rising and going up the chart? As we look at the projection, I see that they did not hold on to hope. They grieved themselves to death. They degenerated. They became dehydrated and died but I, God am the

God of a second chance.

God called him again, Ezekiel, the name given to him at birth. Ezekiel had seen the natural side of God, but when God began to talk to him one on one, encouraging him, He called him, "Son of Man", setting him up to operate in the supernatural power of Him. He asked him, ***"Can these bones live again?"*** Ezekiel responded, "God, only you know the answer because in the beginning was the word and the word was God; And the word dwelt among us and the word became flesh." We are now the word of God in these earthen vessels. God began to allow Ezekiel to see where they were once on the mountain and fell off into the valley.

When God Wants to Lift You and Give You A Second Wind

God asked Ezekiel, "Can these bones live again?" God tested Ezekiel to bring clarification that if you made it through in your mind, seeing death surrounding you, I know you are equipped for this task.

When God wants you to know the power that rest in you when you look back and wonder, "How did I make it through? How did I survive?" It is called remaining hopeful.

A mighty army died out. A mighty army forgot that God existed. A mighty army forgot that God brought them out of bondage. God called Ezekiel to step up and be an investigator and a reporter. Let me empower you with this valuable information. I need you to see how I saw them at the beginning when they were also created in my image and in my power. Ezekiel, I need you to go down into the midst of the valley and tell me what you see.

Sometimes in life we may have to go into the valley of decisions but do not die in your experience. Do not die from a doctor's report. Believe the report of the Lord and ye shall live.

"Ezekiel what is in the valley? Talk back to me. What is in the valley that killed my people?"

God being all knowing already knew but wanted to hear Ezekiel express what he witnessed from his eyes. He witnessed that the army had died in the valley and that they became the place in which they were stuck; the valley of depression, not willing to pull themselves up the upland hills to reach the mountain. We must remember that where there is a valley there is also a mountain. For valleys are surrounded by mountains.

When you become trapped in your mind, Satan will drain you to kill you. Do not die in the valley, feeling abandoned.

O ye nations hear ye the word of the Lord and Live! Hear this alert. Some of the problems that have landed you in the valley today are Loneliness, Rejection, Cancer, High Blood Pressure, and Depression. These problems can take one deeper into the valley of crisis, but Jesus is the answer for the world today. Choose to climb the hills and make it to the mountains. The devil's job is to make you feel empty, battling in your mind with the strongholds of loneliness, rejection, cancer, high blood pressure, and depression. Occupy your position. Live and Not Die. *Let the winds of God lift you back up onto the mountain. You can escape death just as Ezekiel did. Will you be the now Ezekiel, knowing death wants to claim you as you proclaim, "I will not die in the valley"?*

God spoke again unto the son of man, expressing his Agape love. "Ezekiel know that the bones that you are looking at scattered everywhere were once my heart." While they were living, they forgot about the Creator, God. Whatever you do, keep God in the midst.

I would encourage you to live above your circumstance and use your access to the **Kingdom of God**. For we are the beloved of God. Let us not let a nation die. Let us release the authority of prayer. As I speak unto you as being a servant of God, I want to encourage you and say that God will give us a second wind. God will lead us beside the still waters. God is able to restore our souls as he has placed the same authority in our hands to represent His Kingdom, going against any dark force.

We must remember that the race is not given unto the swift neither the battle unto the strong, but it is given unto the one who shall endure unto the end. Let us run the race that is set before us as we push and travail through the thickness of the clouds. Ask

God to give you a second wind. For we are in the race of our lives, looking at death all around us. We must allow the second wind to kick in. Our minds should be set towards the mark of the prize of the high calling of God which is in Christ Jesus. Right there say, *"Lord give us a second wind."*

Some of you may feel as if you cannot see your way but do not die in the valley. Ask God for the second wind. When everything is breaking loose you must endure. As Ezekiel is moving deeper into the valley, he had to kick the scattered bones out of the way for him to make a pathway to be able to investigate as God commanded him to, knowing that he could have been one of the ones that were dead but was *LEFT FOR THE ASSIGNMENT.*

Here we are in the Year of 2020. God began to share with Ezekiel, "I'm going to give Israel one more wind to prove to me that they really love me. I'm going to give them one more wind to see if they trust me."

God expressed to Ezekiel, "My heart is broken but I yet love this army that has died out. What happened to our connection? Who unplugged the cord of the relationship that we once shared? I do not understand how they did not remember all the marvelous works I have done for them and how I brought them out of the house of bondage. Ezekiel, I allowed you to avoid death."

Are there any Ezekiels in the Year of 2020 that are yet Thankful to be alive? Do not allow the money, fortune, and fame of this world to put you in the dry bones category. I promise you that money cannot replace your soul. What does it profit to gain the whole world and lose your soul? Do not die in the valley.

We are going to need the word of God to decree and establish here in the earth realm. For God stands by His word. Do not allow money and the cares of this life to cause you to break God's heart all over again. We must remember that God was the one that sent His only begotten son to bear our grief and our shame, being despised and rejected. He was beaten beyond recognition. There was no glory to look upon Him. He died an ugly death so that we may be healed by His stripes; to be healed, delivered, and set free.

As Ezekiel is in the midst of the valley, God began to orchestrate the movement that was getting ready to take place saying, Prophesy. I can imagine Ezekiel shaking his head as he looked at the dead bones receiving the strength from God as he received the authority to prophesy unto the winds that had to participate in the resurrection of life to resuscitate the dead bones. Ezekiel responded back to God saying, "I need the power of you to speak life."

God said that is why I called you because I knew you were equipped for the journey. While you are standing in the midst of these dry bones COMMAND LIFE. Ezekiel, I need you to collect the dead bones and command the foot bone to connect to the ankle bone, the ankle bone to the leg bone, the leg bone to the knee bone, the knee bone to the thigh bone, the thigh bone to the hip bone, the hip bone to the back bone, the back bone to the neck bone, and the neck bone to the head bone. Ezekiel sees what God made all over again as they bounce back, becoming stronger as God says, "Look at the bones that I allowed you to call together once again."

We are summons before God to call life unto this nation just as Ezekiel was. Even when the army was connected back together, they were yet missing their breath. God allowed Ezekiel to call the four winds into order and command life to re-enter and they became living souls.

There is life when we call the four winds of

God. The air that we breathe represents the life of God. When Ezekiel began to call the winds of God together, a rumbling caused a shaking to take place. Action was being demonstrated from the power of God. Let us come together from the north, the south, the east and the west, causing a rotation to bring forth the manifestation. For when we open our mouths, we release the breath of God which is the winds of God. ***RUMBLE***.

Be Not Weary

PRAYER

Father we thank you for the fire of the Holy ghost. Your word says in Isaiah Chapter 40:31 "But they that wait upon the LORD shall renew their strength; they shall mount up with wings as eagles; they shall run, and not be weary; and they shall walk, and not faint." Father God here it is that we your children come before you as you are our father.

We come giving you glory. We come standing the gap. We come speaking life in the Name of Jesus Christ. Father we thank you as we are worshipping you across the world. We open our mouths and we give you praise because your word says in all things give thanks. As we kneel and lift our hands, we say thank you Lord.

Lord we thank you for the winds of you as we are seeking the manifestation of your glory and of your power. Let us release the spirit of Mordecai. For your word says some things come only by fasting and praying. We are standing for the nation as we are speaking life. You give us the capability to inhale and exhale your power, giving us strength to remain on the walls.

Open your mouth and give God praise as we leap into the glory of God, thanking him for healing, deliverance, and setting free.

Open your mouth and give him a worthy praise. Saturate your home. Saturate your job so that the glory of God will come in. We thank you because you will lift a bowed down head. You will be our hope. You are the rock that we stand on. LORD we thank you for blessing and pouring out your abundance of grace and your abundance of mercy.

We thank you for the energy to come together with the soul and the spirit to intensify the windmills. For we will not be separated. For my soul is in oneness with my spirit.

Our souls fight for the right to live. Thank you for paying attention to our voice.

43

FLOW

PRAYER

By the power that is in the name of Jesus, I come against the spirit of drainage. My water will flow with free course. I will not be dry nor empty. My well is not stopped up. For I have tasted of the living water. Father thank you for the awareness from *Luke 22:31* as I speak knowing that Satan desires to sift me as wheat. I will pay attention.

I will not be caught off-guard. I will use the tool of your word, casting down the strongholds of Satan, in the Name of Jesus. Father we thank you for releasing your anointing upon us that shall multiply our strength. We will not be entangled with the spirit of discord or confusion, that will try to stop our flow. Father we thank you for we are strengthened in the knowledge that Satan wants to drain and sift us as wheat. Our water will continue to flow. We will not be sifted as wheat. Thank you that Jesus's prayer yet covers us from the crown of our heads to the soles of our feet. Father we thank you that we are now strengthened to strengthen our brethren. And it is so in Jesus Name. Amen

Dissipate & Destroy It with

Prayer

WORDS OF EXHORTATION

Whatever you are going through, I heard the Lord say, *"Dissipate & Destroy It."* **at 4:55pm Central Standard Time, Sunday August 23, 2020**. Toss it in the air, releasing it into the winds for God, The Almighty One, to grant His attention unto it.

For stress shall not be a part of my life. I am the person that holds my mind in order. My mind serves the ability to hand over any problems into the hands of the one who is capable to solve them all. I release everything negative unto my Lord & Savior Jesus Christ, as I tell problems to take a hike, as I release prayer to its height. For there is not a problem Jesus cannot solve. He did it when He was slaughtered like a hog. I dissipate as I rejoice for my mind is renewed and strengthened, me being the champion of my mind; lifting the wheels of Ezekiel as he saw God as a wheel in the middle of a wheel. For if there shall be a blow out the spare is always available. For we are connected! Wheels take different paths of traveling this world, picking up one another through the radar from the winds of

God. We will be the endurance, giving out a jump off, not allowing one another's battery to go dead.

We will keep the prayer wheels turning as this world rotates. We are the wheels of prayer. For prayer knows no time zone. It just travels as we send the word to do the work as the wheels are turning! Cars carry four wheels for the weight of each vehicle. We are the culture all in prayer together with different races form all nationalities. Yet and still we are made from our Father who is in Heaven. We are His Kingdom. We cannot be numbered, being the wheel in the middle of the wheel, spreading the actions of the influx of prayer. We release the wheels. *DISSAPPATE.*

Use the Trade Name

PRAYER

Father we first give you thanks for trusting us to be faithful unto the call of duty, being given unto much prayer and supplication. We thank you for allowing us to be the altar of prayer. We say Thank you for being in the will of you as we serve in much prayer, believing that you will do a 360 degree turn for the lives of your people. Prayer will cause us to be in regulation, to cause things to come together in the

Name of Jesus. We will profit by shifting to the call of you. Praying, we will use the trade name that has much power, Jesus in the morning, Jesus in the noon day, Jesus at midnight. For the name of Jesus is released from our mouths. We are the trade winds. For Jesus paid it all at Calvary, giving us power to be economy consumers of prayer. And it is so in Jesus Christ Mighty Name.

Personal Ad

PRAYER

LORD I Thank you for the connection that is between you and I. It is so personal, and I am so grateful for you being concerned about my private life as you care about my emotions and my matters.

Thank you for allowing me to be the main column of your personal ad, featuring me every day of my life.

Thank you for how you divided my red sea for me to walk on dry grounds. Thank you for investing your gifts down on the inside of me. For we are a special dual, formed from your winds, making us the

term of a pair. I love you my Father Forever more, in

Jesus name. Amen.

I Stand Against the Problems That Come with This Life!

For Psalms 91:10 states, "There shall no evil befall thee neither shall any plague com nigh thy dwelling." I hold firm as I bring the action to take cover. For I am the dwelling place where your spirit lives and abides. For the angels of the Lord encamp around us. We reverse the curse of the enemy that came to destroy us in Jesus' Name.

The camp of the Lord is established around us. God will dispatch angels to fight for us. If one loses strength along the way, remember that God matched

you for the problems. ***REST.***

54

For We Are Survivors

WORDS OF EXHORTATION

God will raise up a people that will obey His voice. We will give no place unto the spoils of the devil and his works. *Hallelujah*. We release our tongues of fire.

For you are Lord, God, The King of Kings. For you have been a gift from within, that has called us to live lives of purpose for which we were sent to fight for our rights.

For you are our Messiah, our promised deliverer and we say Thank you for making us a survivor from your death. The strongholds that were sent to kill did not happen. We Thank you for our angels watching over us as we travail day by day.

II Corinthians 4:9 says we may have faced brokenness, rejection, abuse, or failure but we are not destroyed. Pull down the gavel. Jesus's dying made us survivors. Thank you. It allowed us to now be witnesses of the resurrection. ***We survived.***

The Tribe of Prayer

PRAYER

This morning our ears are open to listen and obey your instruction. We worship you for being our Lord, our supplier, our Master, our Provider, and our Helper. As we lift our banners of praise, we draw closer and closer unto you. We come unto thee, humble, with our hearts of Thanksgiving, giving you all of us. Glory and honor be unto you for your power.

Thank you for never rejecting us and always pouring on us. For you have been our rock of ages that we can always hide ourselves in.

We are the tribe of prayer, praying for the world and standing in the rank as soldiers in the Army of The Lord. We are in the line of duty to stand. We also Thank you for moving mountains as we see walls fall just as the walls of Jericho. Lord we Thank you for the increase of favor as we blow the wind of Ezekiel. ***ABBA.***

Rehoboth

REHOBOTH has made room! We will mark this place as the ***REHOBOTH*** fountains of wells. We believe therefore we shall receive new wells of water flowing with plenteousness. We shout ***REHOBOTH*** before your presence Almighty God. For you have caused us to experience and taste the spring waters. We are the spiritual system of life's fullness for purifying the waters. ***REHOBOTH!*** Thank you for our waterfalls of blessings.

Genesis 26:22 says, "And he removed from thence, and digged another well; and for that they strove not: and he called the name of it Rehoboth; and he said for now the Lord hath made room for us and we shall be fruitful in the land."

Father we Thank you for making us fruitful as thou has made room! REHOBOTH!

Jeremiah The Weeping Prophet

PRAYER

As I weep before your throne, I can say worthy is the lamb, weeping as the prophet Jeremiah did for the nation! We ask that you would shine your light down from Heaven upon us as you are among us. We pray against the wages of sin that add death but for the gift of you which adds eternal life forever.

Structure us in your will to build strength and move in prayer while construction is going on.

We send the fire of the Holy spirit just as Jeremiah felt when he wanted to be quite but could not as you revealed unto him your love and connection for your people. Father we will not be quiet. It is out of the question. For our prayers will be remarkable, striking down every weight of the enemy in Jesus Name. Amen.

Arise Warriors

Arise warriors and say, "Yes Lord!" Arise warriors and take your positions. Arise to lift the bar of prayer, speaking life as we hold fast. We are able to release the winds of God to cleanse and make whole. For we are the sets of evidence that summarize prayer.

We arise on the chariots of fire, releasing the whirlwind to shape us into a funnel against violence. We Thank you. For we are founded in prayer. You have caused us to be Generals in the spirit from a mighty God, making mighty people. We use our weapons of force as we say, "Satan you are *DISMANTLED.*"

COMPASS

PRAYER

God, we Thank you for being the compass who has wrapped your loving arms around us. Thank you for dropping our charges making it a story of our past and of our shame. We say you are the greatest thing that ever happened to us. As you hung upon a tree just for us. We Thank you again for laying down your life, calling us your friend, as you have given us the power to function. We also say Thank you because we do not walk without a map. We will release the good news.

We Are the Paddles
Of
Prayer

We have the right to use the blood of Jesus who was slain before the foundation of the world. For the word says you were despised and rejected. There was no glory to look upon you. For you bore our grief and our shame. We thank you Lord for dying on the old rugged cross for the wretched, as we are. We say thank you Lord as we live from the example that you left on record. For we are the windmills, circulating from your breath. Father God we Thank you for being good in the name of Jesus.

We are the paddles of prayer. We are the paddles to push against the trials and tribulations, moving forward as the examples of prayer. We will use the paddles as we travail, pushing as a woman giving birth to a newborn baby. Jesus's death gave us life. We will push. We will not become weak along the way. For we are the paddles to go against the waves of the ocean.

We represent you Lord to move our boat forward as we use the paddles, using our strength from the inside of the boat. The boat will not sink. The boat will not go under. The boat will not crash. For we will yet paddle. We will yet keep our vision.

We will keep our strength renewed, representing the power of prayer. We represent the paddles strength to move forward as we have strength to speak a word. For we are the paddles to go against the water.

S.O.S

WORDS OF EXHORTATION

We are the soul of our ships. We sail into the Glory of God, using the code of access of ***Psalm 120:1, A Song of Degrees.*** "In my distress I cried unto the Lord, and he heard me and delivered my soul." I am in operation of my soul as my soul shouts out unto God, signaling in that I have an emergency. For I know that I can call on you **24/7** and **365 days**, any time of day or night.

You are my mayday. For in my distress, I can radio in. Thank you for being the one who takes off the pressures of life. Thank you for the relationship that will show up in my distress. For we are good, the children of God standing strong.

BREATHE

A PROCLOMATION

I can breathe. I will breathe. Satan has no permission to cross the bloodline. I can breathe in his face. My mind is clear. I take the Ruah of God to blow against you and your work. For I am the greater work of God. I am the presentation of the winds of God. Everything about me walks hand in hand, being the produced voice, speech, and sound from God. I have the outgoing winds through my speech, protected with the whole armor of God, to be able to stand firm on His sure foundation. I am the tongue that controls my direction with speech. I stand for the standards of God. Satan you have no authority to enter into my space. For my body belongs to God. The blood of Jesus forever stands against you. I am the reproduced copyright material from Heaven. *I choose to breathe.*

The Prayer of The

Hurricane

Hallelujah Jesus! We charge Heaven. We bombard Heaven. We echo into the Heavens. We worship you for who you are in Heaven. Hallowed be thy name O God. We give ourselves to you and to the inner presence of your glory God. We Thank you for being able to walk it out, to pray it out, to shout it out. Glory be to your name God.

We reverence you here in the earth as we escalate in the spirit realm with you Lord Jesus.

We Thank you as we release the fire of the Holy ghost. For the Holy ghost knows how to take us into the inner courts of you. We will be the Levites that will stand up and worship in your presence. We Thank you for being able to clap our hands, praising you. We take our feet and begin to leap into the presence of you for joy. For the joy of the Lord is our strength. We are charged from the fire of the Holy ghost within to leap. We leap into the glory realm of you. For in your presence is joy. Lord Thank you for the joy of the Holy ghost as we pray in the presence of you the Almighty God.

The world needs you. The world needs your presence. Lord I pray by your spirit that we would seek the God of Abraham. We will seek the God of

Isaac, Jacob, and Israel. We will seek the God that Joseph stood up for. We will seek the God that Moses met on the back side of the dessert. We will seek the God that Gilead and the three hundred knew, being commanded to just make a sound into the heavens. God, we release your glory to do what no other can do. We Thank you as we trust the God that Esther knew. We Thank you as we trust the God that Deborah and Barak knew. We trust the God that Isaiah saw through the scopes of time. We trust the God that called Jeremiah while he was in his mother's belly.

We trust the God that David knew, that caused him to be a warrior. We trust the God that answered by fire when Elijah called Him. We trust the God that called Ezekiel to prophesy unto the four winds. We trust in thee O God. We trust the God that never slumbers nor sleeps. We trust the God that has been here from everlasting unto everlasting. We trust the God that John knew on his Island of Patmos. We trust the God that is in the *NOW* Generation. For we will know you as God as we place our hand in your hands, the Lord God Almighty, who can still the waters.

Lord we Thank you for favor in the earth. We Thank you for being able to call life to a dead situation. ***We trust in you O God! We trust in you O God!*** And we give you glory. In the name of the Lord Jesus, we prophesy health. We prophesy the will of you and the divine glory of you that will shift a nation. We charge our words to travel and to defeat every attack of the enemy. *In the mighty name of Jesus, we trust you God. We trust you God. God, we trust you to do a SUDDENLY making wells of water.*

Elements of The Air

PRAYER

When we pray, we reign with you God as we sit in Heavenly places with you Christ Jesus. We are the substance that is coated with your righteousness. We come into the solid presence of you, being made by you. Therefore, we are able to touch you from within, being made up from the elements of the air that we breathe. For what is within us shall outwardly manifest the changes that make the instance to come alive, becoming the example of God. We bow to the King. We are children of the King.

God Will Supply

WORDS OF EXHORTATION

Give God a response. Say something to God so God can legally move in on your behalf. We must remember that God always responds to His word. We must be attached to the tabernacle of God to receive the attention to our special needs. ***The action to show forth reaction favorably***. We must remember that if God done it before, he will do it again. We are His stimulus of the verb of action. Not only will God reply but He will also supply. If we call Him, He will answer us. His availability is available without standing in a long line. God will reply to the charge of our case, being our defense.

Jehovah Jireh will be placed in our location to free our minds. We will not live the life of a defeated army. We will rise up just as Jehoshaphat. We will not worry. We will trust God.

The Prayer of Travail

HALLELUJAH TO YOU BE THE GLORY. HALLELUJAH TO YOU BE THE GLORY LORD. HALLELUJAH TO YOU BE ALL THE GLORY. ALL THE GLORY BELONGS TO YOU O GOD.

YES God! We enter your gates with thanksgiving. We honor you for being the Lord God Almighty, The Everlasting God, The Prince and The Peace. We enter the inner courts of you God.

We worship you with our lips. We lift our hands and say worthy are you God. We Thank you for the baptism of the Holy ghost. We Thank you for the indwelling of your spirit. We Thank you as we accelerate into the spirit zone with you. We Thank you because we are able to inhale and exhale you. We worship you with our lips. For our lips were created to worship you, The Almighty God, The everlasting One, The Messiah, The Emmanuel, God in us, and God among us. We worship you for your greatness. We Thank you for being Lord over our lives. We thank you as we lay before your presence. We bring ourselves as a living sacrifice, holy and acceptable unto you. For this is our reasonable service. We owe you our worship.

We owe you our praise. We owe you for just giving us life. We thank you for the breath that we breathe.

We thank you for the Holy spirit that enlightens us and empowers us to be equipped for every journey that is set before us. We do not take life for granted. We stand in the liberty of your mind and the freedom to speak from the Winds of God as you pour your oil deep down within us. We thank you because we are on an assignment to pray and to seek your mind as never before.

Even as we pray for this pandemic right now, we command it to cease in the name of Jesus Christ. We come against the spirit of rebelliousness in the name of Jesus that wants to buck against your word. You have commanded us to pray according to *II Chronicles 7:14.* We are your people that have been called by Your Name to exercise our gifts and to exercise our faith that moves us from Glory to Glory as we speak from your mouth, touching and agreeing with one accord; being in the mind of you, being in the mindset to pray, and being in the mindset to seek you God. We thank you for a free will to worship you with our lips. In the name of the Lord Jesus. We do not take life granted. We thank you for keeping us from dangers seen and unseen. We know that you are a prayer answering God. We thank you as we touch and agree with the heavenly host. In the name of Jesus, we stretch out on your word. You stretched this world out on your word. We stand on the winds of your breath as we speak with you being our Father who is so concerned about us here in the earth realm. In the name of Jesus send forth the Ruah, your breath, as never before to crush this pandemic, this Covid-19 in the name of Jesus Christ.

We ask that you would move in the schools in The Name of Jesus. We ask that you would cover the teachers and that you would cover the students, in The Name of Jesus. We ask that you would go into the hospitals, the nursing homes, and that you would bless the doctors, the nurses, and everyone that is playing their part.

We have been called to play our part in the earth and that is to pray with the winds of you and to stand in the authority of Jesus Christ. Your word says that we will see the goodness of you Lord in the land of the living. For our souls panteth after thee O God. We are thirsty for your righteousness.

For you are our righteousness. In the name of Jesus, we will pray. We will seek you. We will call upon the name of the Lord in the name of Jesus. Even as we speak, we pull down strongholds. We apply the blood. Your blood travails! Your blood travails! Your blood travails!

We will pray until our Heavenly language changes. We will pray until you take us to different dimensions. We will pray with your resurrection power. We will pray, giving Thanks always, with much prayer and much supplication.

We will pray to see mountains be removed. We will pray to see you in your full glory and your power. Everything that is not in order with you we come against it by the power that is in the name of

Jesus. We command by the authority that is in the name of Jesus and we pray that whatever is going on behind the scenes that it will be revealed. We come against the iron angel in the name of Jesus. We will hold fast unto the altar of prayer. We will lay ourselves before you. For you are the fountain that is able to fill us. We will press the oil to pray as we accelerate into the spirit realm. We will blow your trumpets O God. We will not be weary in well doing. We will not give in. We will worship you in spirit and in truth. ***I hear the spirit saying come on Zion, worship God.***

We worship you for your goodness and your mercy unto us. Your track record is beyond this world. From John the Baptist until now we have suffered violence and we speak against this pandemic and we speak against the air that has been polluted, in the name of Jesus Christ. Lord God we thank you for breathing of the fresh winds of you God. We will compass and we will travail. We will see the goodness of you in the mighty name of Jesus. For you are the God that is for us.

If God be for us who can be against us as we stand the gap on the walls praying. Your word says when Zion travailed Judah came forth and we will praise you Lord. We thank you for the shifting that is taking place in the earth realm for your glory. For your understanding and for your glory. For your glory God!

As we are touching you God, you are touching

our mind. As we are touching you Lord, you are touching our hearts. We speak the supernatural healing of you. Everything that we are going through and everything that we are faced with, it was defeated, derailed, and dethroned at the cross of calvary. We call for the blood. The blood. The blood. The blood covers all fifty states and all the continents. We raise the bar up to you God and we give you glory because we know you will answer. We trust you in the Year of 2020. For iron sharpens iron.

We have been called to seek you. We have been called to pray. We are pushing and travailing and we are trusting you. We give you glory even in the midst of a crisis and in the midst of a pandemic.

We you give you glory because you walk with us and you talk with us. You tell us that we are your own. *We will give your name the glory. And we give you Glory! And we give you glory! Henceforth now and forever more as we rest in the presence of you.*

We cover our families under the blood of Jesus. We command our bloodline to line up. We command our bloodline to be safe. We command our bloodline to be healed. We command our bloodline to come forth in the name of Jesus Christ and we will see you in your glory in the name of Jesus as we enter the floodgates of your great power. For we come to do battle. We seek you God. We speak against the darkness that has covered this world in the name of Jesus. You said in the beginning, "Let there be light." and I speak the light of you Jesus. I speak light in this darkness, in the mighty name of Jesus. For you are God and you work miracles. Miracles are yet to be performed to bring your name glory. We clear the way for you to enter in as we shout Hosanna to the Most High God. We give you the glory God. We give you the glory God.

We give you the glory God. Rehoboth! You will make room for us. You will give wells of water. Our waters will not run dry. We will drink of the goodness of you. We will tell of the grace of you. We Thank you for covering us under your blood. ***And it is so. And it is so. And it is so! As your word travels.*** It has traveled from time, from the beginning from your mouth and it is now at us and we speak the same word, in The Name of Jesus. We speak; be healed, be delivered, be set free, be refreshed by the renewing of your mind. As we put on the whole armor of you, we will stand, and we will travail as we are traveling through time. ***And we give you glory. We give you glory. We give you glory!*** We live in the divine will of you and we thank you for the abundance of rain. We decree and declare that the devil is defeated, he is confused, and he is discombobulated.

We come against the witches and warlocks. We come against spiritual wickedness in high places. We root it out in the name of Jesus Christ, and it is so by your word; And we bless your name O God. We let the tongues of fire go forth and we give you glory Lord. We breathe the fresh winds of you God. We breathe the glory of you. We cannot sleep. We must travail in prayer. We must seek your glory and your power.

I hear the lord saying I am seeking worship.

O God we worship you Lord God. We reign, We reign, We reign!

For we have all been called to pray with the winds of you God.

Being in Position

WORDS OF ENCOURAGEMENT

Let us be in position, being living epistles, that people would want to come and inquire about the God from Heaven that we serve. In *Joshua Chapter 6* it deals with the Walls of Jericho and how God had a leader, a General, in position to put the people in order to see the movement of God, being faced with the Walls of Jericho.

Where is the Joshua Generation?

God assured Joshua, "Just as I was with Moses, so shall I be with thee." ***When you are the next leader to step in position, you are not afraid because you have witnessed what God could do upon leaving Egypt.***

Are you in position to where people will want to know about this great God that you talk about and how you have experienced Him causing your walls of Jericho to fall down flat, and how when you receive a word from Him, you do not doubt it but you stand on it? ***I have a rapport with God.***

As we go to ***Joshua Chapter 6***, it says how Jericho was shut up because of the Children of Israel. None went out and none came in.

In life we will have trials and tribulations that

go with the process of life. There is a time and a season for all things under the sun but while you are going through make sure that you access patience while facing your "Walls of Jericho". When the enemy tries to bring in doubt, reject it.

Stay in position to hear God concerning your walls of Jericho. We are the priest in position to move the Ark of the Covenant. We must remember the same God that was with Joshua is with us today in our process. For He is the same God yesterday, today, and forever more. Joshua made sure that the people were in order, being able to carry out the assignment that God had placed upon them. Let us make sure that our lives are in order that the glory of God may be revealed.

The priest were the ones who were chosen to handle the Ark of the Covenant along with the assignment to blow the trumpet for the people to shout with a great shout. God has placed all that we need in our mouths. Take a moment with you being the priest over your affairs and begin to shout and echo into the Heavens as you are moving in faith to see the resurrection power of Jesus Christ. For we hold the ark of God.

Our Praise is Our Trumpet.

*When **God releases you to dance even in the midst of crisis**, when you are a **warrior**, when you are an **intercessor**, and most of all **when you know God and God knows you**, you have the power to march around the walls of Jericho. Do not get tired and do not be weary while looking at your walls.*

March around your walls of Jericho!

Release doubt, release fear, *and* ***stand in the liberty of God!***

As the Children of Israel were approaching the seventh day, they were preparing for the battle to release the double portion. They were shifting to both march and take action. On the seventh day, they had to march around the wall seven times, and they could not get tired of the assignment that God had already said they would ***CONQUER***!

We must pray as never before. We must remain on the wall until God commands us to shout with the voice of triumph. For we will come through and we will see the glory of God in the land of the living. Joshua and the Children of Israel travailed.

The only thing God wanted them to do was to go in and take what was rightfully theirs. From John the Baptist even to now the Kingdom of God has suffered violence and we take it by force!

Joshua could not have Priest who were fearful. By the spirit I can assure you that these Priest are the same ones who stepped in the Muddy Jordan. What kind of rhythm does Satan see that you have with God? Does Satan see that you are going to trust God or does Satan see that you are getting weary and can go to God to accuse you saying, "They are getting weary now?!"

The word of the Lord says some trust in chariots and some trust in horses, but we will trust in the Name of The LORD. They had to burn down the place called Jericho. The only thing that God wanted was what belonged to them. Someone may have something that belongs to you but are you willing to march and are you willing to pray until you see your faith take a quantum leap; until you **PUSH &TRAVAIL** to move them out of the place that God has already said belongs to you? For we must remember that the battle is not ours, but our battles belong to God.

We take courage in knowing that God is God and that all we have to do is release the winds of God. That is what Israel did. They released a sound. We do not always know which direction the wind is coming from, but we feel it and that is the way our prayer life should be, like the winds of God! We are supposed to be able to ambush the enemy. We are supposed to pray until we see action here in the earth realm.

We Shall be Stable

PRAYER

Thank you, Jesus. For you are our strength God. Thank you, Jesus. For you are our mind regulator. Thank you, Jesus that we can unload our burdens upon you O God. Thank you, Jesus that we can bring every one of our concerns before you and leave them at the feet of you. For your word says cast all your cares upon the Lord for He cares for you. We release stress. We release every spirit that would try to attach itself. For no spirit will live or rest upon us but the spirit of you, The Almighty

God. We will not become fretful. We will not be intimidated. We will not, not fight. We will stand in the liberty of your power. We take the freedom of our mind, made from the liberty of you God, that shifted us into this world to make a domino effect and we say Thank you O God! And we give you praise! We love you! And we magnify you! For we shall be stable in the name of the Lord Jesus Christ of Nazareth. We represent grace. We represent favor. We represent your mercy. We represent your anointing and your power. We represent the manifestation of your will. You have a will, a purpose, and a plan for our lives. As we step up to the scope, we will look beyond what we are faced with and we will trust the process of you O God.

We give you PRAISE. We give you GLORY. We give you HONOR. We rest in Heavenly places with you Christ Jesus and we Thank you for the Holy ghost that gives intercession for us. We can groan before you. We can hum before your presence. We can release ourselves in the presence of you and we can become unglued because you are the God who is able to put us back together again. We Thank you for the spirit of Jeremiah. For the spirit releases the fire to go against the principalities of the fiery darts. We say Thank you God because it is so! We are renewed in our minds. We are strengthened. We will fight the good fight of faith, leaning and depending upon you The Almighty God.

WORDS OF

ENLIGHTENMENT

God has given us a choice. "Behold I set before you good and evil, you choose." Be aware in the consciousness of your mind that God does not tempt man. Be empowered. It is the enemy's job to tempt you, to cause you to doubt and not trust God. We are living in a time now and God began to speak to me. Will you have an ear to hear what the spirit of the Lord is speaking? According to the word of the Lord, we have the authority to take our heels even now with what is going on and bruise the serpents head, according to *Genesis 3:15*.

God said that this is a comeback for the believers. Where Satan came in like a flood, the spirit of the Lord lifted a standard. I asked God, "What is it about the heel?" God said, "The heel of the shoe makes the shoe step high." In the time and the season that we are living in, we are supposed to be marching high, showing the strength of God.

I pray that the believers will come on and take your place. *STAND GUARD*. We do not have to be in the church. For we are the temple of the Most High God. Let us get in our place and in our rank. Let us stir up the gifts that remain and hear God as never before so that we will see the glory of God.

God said I am calling for the believers to worship me. There is a difference between your worship and your praise. Your worship brings down the Shekinah glory. It is something about your worship. It tells God how much you appreciate Him and how much you love Him and takes you behind the veil. Do you not know that the veil was rent so that we could have permission to go into the inner courts in a time like this in our life to pull down any pandemic? And we decree from the mouth of the Lord God Almighty that we will fear God and stretch out on him.

God adopted us in. That is agape love. That is unconditional love. Loving yourself is loving God.

You meet yourself when you meet the creator down on the inside of you. He will love you like no other and stick closer than a brother. His name is Jesus. We welcome the Shekinah glory of God's presence. Come on and go behind the veil.

GRACE

PRAYER

We worship you Lord. We worship you Lord. We worship Lord because you have been good. You have made ways out of no ways. You took our mourning and you turned it into dancing. For the spirit of heaviness, you sent an angel to wrap us with a garment of praise. When we think back over our lives and where you have brought us from and where we are today, we know it has been your grace. When we should have lost our minds and when we should have been cast down, when we were forsaken, you lifted us up. We Thank you Lord for your grace. For you are the King of Glory. You are the Lord God Almighty. You are mighty in battle. You are the Great I Am. You are the Lily of the Valley. You are the Lord our Shepard and we shall not want for anything. You lead us beside the still waters. We command ***STILL WATERS*** in the name of Jesus.

We thank you God as we are walking through muddy Jordan. For we are the priest that bear the ark of the covenant. We do not walk in fear, but we march to the rhythm of your beat. We worship, we magnify you, and we exalt you.

Will you give Him a yes Lord to your will and your way and seek His mind? We are able to go into the inner courts with God because the invitation was given over two thousand years ago. We go into the inner courts of God. It is something about when the Levites begin to worship God and tell Him how great He is and how many doors He has opened, How He blocked things and made death behave. ***THE GRACE OF GOD.*** How He died on the cross and how He was despised and rejected. ***HE HAS BEEN GOOD AND THAT IS WHY WE OWE HIM OUR ALL. GRACE.***

We worship your glory. We worship your glory. I heard the Lord say, "I am calling my people into pure worship. For I am a pure God."

God can do what man cannot do. He can purify. He can make us brand new. He can heal. He can deliver. He can set **FREE**. He can open doors, but we have to use the authorities of the keys that are in His word.

~Trust in the Lord with all your heart and lean not unto your own understanding. Will you really acknowledge God? Do you really have faith to believe God? Let us give God honor for His grace.

CONQUERING AGAINST ALL ODDS

Romans 8:37 states; "Nay, in all these things we are more than conquerors through him that loved us." **II Corinthians 4:9** says, "Persecuted, but not forsaken; cast down, but not destroyed." We will survive. We will bounce back. We will dismiss the shocks. We are conquerors. I pray that my personal testimony will serve as a witness that God has the last say. The world styled me as being illiterate. I graduated with a 1.06, Grade Point Average, but I and you can do all things through Christ which strengthens us. I beat the odds. I am a miracle. When all else failed me, I tried God. I am a witness that God does hear and answer prayer. This is my sixth book, writing from the supernatural power of God, no ghost-writer, nothing but the Holy ghost. May God bless the whole wide world.

ARE YOU A REPEAT OF YOUR GENERATION?

Have you been sabotaged? Are you the victim of a generational curse? Have you ever wondered, "Why am I here? Why do cycles repeat themselves in my life?" There is a hidden assassination attempt on your life by the enemy. However, God is a concerned God who wants to bring us into the full development and knowledge of who we are. The experiences we have in life shape us for better or worse. God wants us to stand steadfast in the liberty he has given us and root our identities in Him. Its's time to move forward and break the cycle!

AVAILABLE ON www.lisapoeministries.wordpress.com, www.amazon.com www.walmart.com www.barnesandnoble.com www.booksamillion.com www.alibris.com

FOR A SIGNED COPY OR MORE INFORMATION YOU MAY CALL 855-444-RUAH (7824)

HERE ON PURPOSE NOT BY ACCIDENT

I understand in life we are not all the same, different calibers of life, with different life stories. There is a reason and purpose why we exist. You are not a mistake or misfit. You are a treasure worth seeking for. Have you come into the realization of who you are? Coming into the realization of who you are, there is a need for you to be fully aware that you are a powerful factor to the factory of the economy structure. Build up, Structure up, now Speak up; "I am here with purpose, living out the energy that has been invested within, shifting this world with the domino effect!"

AVAILABLE ON www.lisapoeministries.wordpress.com, www.amazon.com www.barnesandnoble.com, www.booksamillion.com and Other Retailers

FOR A SIGNED COPY OR MORE INFORMATION YOU MAY CALL 855-444-RUAH (7824)

BREAKING THE DEVIL'S CODES

WHO IS BEHIND THE SCENE OF THE CHAOS, CONFUSION, SEPERATION, AND HATRED THAT'S MOVING THROUGHOUT THE LAND, RELEASING, AND IMPOUNDING DISORDER? I WANT TO BREAK THE SILENCE AND ALARM YOU THAT RECESS IS OVER.WAKE UP. THERE IS A MECHANISM SYSTEM PROGRAM CALLED DECEITFULNESS IN PLACE WITH METHODICAL SCHEMES THAT'S PLOTTING AGAINST YOUR LIFE AND WANTS TO DRAG YOUR CHARACTER DOWN TO ZERO BALANCE. WHO IS BEHIND ALL THE MURDERING AND MENTAL ILLNESS? WHO IS WAGING WAR AGAINST YOU AND YOUR FAMILY?

AVAILABLE ON: www.lisapoeministries.wordpress.com, amazon.com IN Paperback or e-Book, barnesandnoble.com, booksamillion.com,walmart .com, & Other Retailers

FOR A SIGNED COPY OR MORE INFORMATION YOU MAY
CALL 855-444-RUAH (7824)

THE YEAR OF EYES HAVEN'T SEEN 2020

Becoming impaired with a plague that has hit the Year of 2020, causing much disfunction, being faced with a virus called COVID-19, making people paranoid, not being able to see through the scope as we approached this Year of Eyes Haven't Seen, the Collision hit like that of a 9-1-1 called COVID-19; when a pandemic hits a whole world and places a whole world at a standstill with people's minds running at a rate of high, not being aware that life can change Oh So Suddenly. For the Year of 2020 is the mystery that puzzled the mind of many people, a crisis causing people's emotions to run at a high, high rate, being fearfully afraid of a world shutting down SUDDENLY, without warning or hesitation. For we are in the Year of Eyes Haven't Seen, as this widespread plague hit as hard as a rock, shattering a window, and causing disfunction, introducing itself as COVID-19, like a 9-1-1 emergency, spreading like a wildfire. God bless the world. If you want to know the time that we are living in, we're living in the SUDDENLY.

AVAILABLE ON: www.lisapoeministries.wordpress.com, amazon.com IN Paperback or e-Book, barnesandnoble.com, booksamillion.com,walmart .com, & Other Retailers

FOR A SIGNED COPY OR MORE INFORMATION YOU MAY CALL
855-444-RUAH (7824)

THE FIRE OF THE SOLAR PRAYER BOOK

We are now the SOLAR of the earth, the radiation that releases the sun to shine in a blackout, using the rotation to send out our high VOLTS that can cause a movement as we thrust the power of prayer, and as we will address our words to have action here in the earth realm. For we are the circle of the SOLAR. For God has given us dominion and power here in the earth. We will shadow the earth with much prayer, being the electricity of the SOLAR SYSTEM

AVAILABLE ON: www.lisapoeministries.wordpress.com, amazon.com IN Paperback or e-Book, barnesandnoble.com, booksamillion.com,walmart .com, & Other Retailers

FOR A SIGNED COPY OR MORE INFORMATION YOU MAY CALL 855-444-RUAH (7824)

RUAH THE BREATH OF GOD, LLC.™
CLOTHING & APPARREL

**FOR ORDERING INFORMATION
CONTACT
RUAH THE BREATH OF GOD,
LLC.
855-444-RUAH (7824)**

Made in the USA
Monee, IL
08 July 2026

56550985R00069